There Sl

Poetry About Life and Love, People and Places

Mary Hurlbut Cordier

Mary Hurlbut Cordier

ISBN: 9798788428017
Imprint: Independently published

Cover photo "Grand Tetons Sunset," by Mary Hurlbut Cordier.
Author photo by Janice Grand.

Technical assistance by Forest Gluys.

Dedicated to Sherwood S. Cordier,
1929-2018,
husband and best friend.

Table of Contents

There Should Be Stars

There should be stars and perhaps a planet or two
and definitely moon glow to celebrate this journey
begun *here* with spilled coffee at that picnic
and circling the world toward *eternity*.

Who knew that stars were within
our reach from the mountain tops,
and glowing in the silver pathways across the lake,
along the wind blown beaches of summer,
through the startling beauty of spring's resurrection,
the poignant autumn songs, and
the star-filled snows of winter.

There should be sunshine to guide our way
as castles and cathedrals cast their light
demanding that we learn from the past
but live in the present and shape the future.
The mountains and fjords of the north countries,
the heartland's prairies and plains,
each spilled their histories, people,
and places in the world onto our pages.

There should be radiance throughout our memories
as we cope with triumphs of the next generations,
now grown beyond the confines of our keeping.
There will be rain and clouds to remind us
as one bright light fades too soon,
the steadfast stars remain upholding the glow of life.

There must be music every day,
a fontana of sounds, a new symphony,
the swan's flight, a magical clarinet,
the soothing sax, and songs to sing
while the windsong shimmers in the pines
and the robin's evensong
brings music into our souls.

There is love in remembrance,
in repose, and sharing a glass of wine,
a walk in the woods, and a family dinner
shared through celebrations and joy,
through compassion and strength.
There should be stars to lead our way.
There will be our stars.

Winter Sun

Winter sunshine warms my face,
the overstuffed rocking chair surrounds me,
tucked under that ugly green quilt.
My sore throat waits for green tea and toast
and my mother's warm hands
as the opera ascends from the square brown radio,
tiny people inside singing the sad songs of La Bohéme.

That little house is still a home,
the pasture, bereft of horses, overflowing with houses.
Could there be another sunny rocking chair
protecting a child while Mimi longs for spring,
warmed by Rodolfo's hands?

Now, my faraway window frames
sunlit pines, pink in the morning light.
Somewhere near, the deer are watching,
waiting for my green hostas,
free lunch with a birdbath chaser.

Sibelius surrounds and saturates my sun and shadows
and I am warmed by my old love's hands
as we watch for verdant spring and the deer.

When I Think of Home

When I think of home,
I hold dear the sparkling light on the lake,
the steady heartbeat of waves on the shore,
the woods, the creek, that majestic oak,
the fresh-plowed loam.

Home is the earth,
mine to cherish and protect,
my peaceful and loving haven.
Home is where my heart is.

When I think about home
I just want to smile.
This is where I can be me,
where I am accepted for who I am.

Home is a feeling,
not just a place.
Here happy faces and my dog welcome me.
There's a fire in the fireplace and a cat on my lap.

When I think of home
I can almost smell the fresh-baked chocolate-chip
cookies,
chicken and dumplings, home-canned peaches,
a kettle of soup and hot coffee to share around
the table.

Home is my boundless family,
my sisters, my mother, dad and the boys,
my children, wherever they are, my dear spouse.
Here I am blessed with music and laughter.

When I think of home
I mourn the loss of time and place,
the wonder and sunshine of my youth,
my lost loved ones.

Home is sweet memories
of my far away home
recalled with a wistful smile and love,
claimed by the past and forever in my heart.

When I think about home
I just want to stay there, wrapped in patience and love.
Here is my warm, comforting place to come
while looking forward with hope and courage.

Home is an anchor
so I won't get lost in this tumultuous sea,
so I know where and who I am.
Home is my anchor of love.

Continuum

Middle-age, they call it.
Half-way there or
half-way finished?
Spread in the middle,
squeezed from both sides!

Might there have been a better term
to spur us on
and cheer our way?
A euphemistic way of saying
we've come a long way?

Ah me! Perhaps the next generation
shall invent that lovely word or phrase
that makes us pleased and proud to say
I'm in the middle!
I'm strong enough to hold the aged,
guide the young and know myself.

Sentinels

Over my head, on a spring morning,
I hear music in the air.
Robins and redwings,
the sentinels of spring,
are clearing the cobwebs of winter
with their flourishing noise,
a seeming celebration of
earth's inevitable cycles.

The chatty chickadee, my favorite,
cautions me that the bird feeder is empty.
I wonder why that tiny being
landed on the book I was reading,
and for a brief exhilarating moment
we were eye-to-astonished eye.

On the lakeshore, the seagulls
argue and curse each other.
They shriek their raucous warnings
as they snatch a share of my picnic,

then swoop and glide with elegance
over the blue waves,
ignoring the sand-castled children.

The canary in the coal mine,
that caged early-warning system,
a far cry from the tiny yellow fluff balls
my grandmother nurtured
in her dining room aviary.
Bursting bubbles of song, their sentinel call.
They didn't know they were captives.

Sadly unseen, except for the losers,
the sky-born sentries tilt with windmills,
search the vanquished forest,
and flee the oil-spoiled river.
I watch the city geese follow-the-leader
and hope they will fly out of hurried harms' way.

Those sentinels of the lakeshore,
the forest and city, my backyard guardians—

their songs and flight bring word and
wisdom to my earth-bound journey
through the warp and weft of sight and sound.
Through their bursts of feathered color,
I learn to treasure these familiar songs,
these reminders of my humanity.

Poor Robin

The North Wind doth blow
and everyone knows
that means more snow.
Here's this poor bird,
she hasn't heard
the South is preferred
'til the sun says "Go!"

Robin sits in a barn.
She was not warned
it's really not warm.
No wonder she hides
and tries to abide,
with wings at her side
she's only lukewarm.

Fog at My Door

There's fog at my door, quietly gray.
I listen but the morning birds have no song.
The backyard dog's plaintive greeting
is smothered in the secret stillness.

In the quiet, dour fog at the door,
the golden-crowned maple
is a silent sentinel, standing guard,
watching for some glimmer of warmth.

As the fog engulfs my spirits,
I long for a summer day's benevolence.
Hidden in my somber surroundings
is there a swirl of light and sound ?

I listen as I warily open the door.
The backyard dog announces a new glow.
Perhaps my diverse plans and dreams
can now sift through the fading gloom.

The Darkening Sky

In the darkening sky,
upheld by spring-green trees,
a circling hawk glides gracefully
on the unseen thermals.
Redwing's burbling aria accents
Robin's gentle evensong.

Soon the Great Bear
will amble around Polaris
as Orion dons his shining belt,
ready for the celestial hunt.
And Cassiopeia in all
her self-proclaimed beauty
clings to her swirling aerial throne.

Memories of bird song linger
as the sky stories fade away,
dimmed by Milky Way pretenders.

Earthbound city lights,
have killed these distant denizens,
their remains hidden in secret darkness.

Perhaps that was a vulture
sailing on the twilight winds.

Adventure

I watch a giant, pale blue spaceship
streaking out-bound to the heavens,
carrying space-garbed tourists,
eager for their weightless minutes.
What an adventure,
          so far from earth.

I wonder what they are looking for,
what they expect to see or do,
          so far from earth.
Are they hoping to confirm that
heaven is accessible and easier to enter
than pushing a camel through the needle's eye?
Are they searching for the swirling colors
astronomers share with us earthlings?
Will they have an ethereal view of the universe
and a festive time floating in space,
          so far from earth?

The giant Webb telescope is out-bound
on its million-mile search of space,

I wonder what will be found as it explores
the universe and orbits our Sun.
Will it observe the origins of the galaxies?
What an adventure,
so far from earth.

Carved on a bench by the lake,
there's a lonely lover's message,
Wait for me in the stars,
so far from earth.
I wonder if their stellar reunion
is accessible out there in the stars.
They won't need Polaris to guide them,
so far from earth.
Their stars are in their hearts.
What an adventure!

Solstice

Our ancient ancestors marked midsummer
with light streaming through rock forms
and doorways, across grand circles,
graves, and mountain tops.
They knew that the solstice was special,
a celestial and seasonal marvel
when the globe is immersed in sunlight.

The warm winds of a summer's night
mark the solstice in our lives
as we celebrate the light of friendship
and marvel at the renewal of the earth
in the lives of our progeny,
circled with flowers and the trees
that shade our reverie.

Could this summer solstice be the time
to consider the wonder of hope?

A time to celebrate the light streaming
across grand circles and mountain tops,
expanding, including, seeking
the beauty of all humankind.

Domain

I quest onward
to sky the mountains,
thought-jammed and breathless,
to sing of waterfalls.

My second roots
are in the endless sand,
journeys and prairies long lost
in the archives of my life.

The lake calls me
to this home of my heart
where pines chant
of wind and wonder.

Lake Song

On a golden day,
children and waves dance
with gulls along the shore
following the silver path of light
on ever-changing blue-green water.
Here the pines sing
and the worldly wind
breathes clear lake air.

Above—endless sky,
the ethereal route to
countless stars and galaxies.
Within—infinite memories,
shining hopes, and knowledge
that through waves and wonder,
we are part of the universe.

Baptism

My daughters are mothers now.
Their daughters see and seek
every corner of the world as their own.

I remember the corners we explored,
my daughters and I--
the butterfly set free,
a tiger swallowtail for the forest.
The wounded hummingbird
held in our hands
a shimmering moment
to fly once more.
The puppies we loved who grew old
and left us to mourn.
Seeds planted and violet bouquets.

Journeys to castles and mountains and plains,
rocks and shells carefully carried home
from the shores of Lake Michigan,
while childhood escaped with the dusk.

Amid our metamorphoses
the lakeshore remains.
On this summer day, once again
the daughters of the Earth are baptized
in the rolling blue-green waters.

Summer Song

I.

On this balmy, star-lit evening,
the frogs are singing their summer song.
The katydids and cicadas join in
celebrating the sunny season's warmth.

Do they dance around the pond at night
rejoicing their summer survival?
Do they know that winter will come again?
Do they read the stars and know what's next?

I listen to their music with wonder:
How did my summer songs slip away
leaving undanced music and empty memories?
Must I wait for the stars to tell my next story?

Summer Song

II.

As the summer songs get louder,
I listen to the music with wonder.
Did the warm, booming rainfall
transform these singing creatures?
Have they increased in number?
Have they grown much larger?
Let's not meet a giant preying mantis.
But not to worry, not to fret,
evolutionary changes are slow to manifest.
But listen—something is scratching,
at my third-floor window.

Tomorrow

This January morning eases in, grim and bleak,
rain-gray and hovering over the swaying spruce.
And here I am, quilt-warm and snug,
reaching for comfort in this new place.
My third floor windows frame my striving plants
stretching toward an unaccustomed sky.

Here is my desk, surrounded by boxes labeled "office."
There, on an unfamiliar shelf, are my books to be read.
Prospective quilts lie waiting in stacks of fabrics.
There are letters to write, bills to be paid,
messages to answer, new friends and old to be greeted,
and a few more boxes to be excavated.

But here I sit with my warmed-over thoughts,
old times, old loves and old lives.
Ah, how memories stir longing and wondering,
making a brew of yesterday and tomorrow.
And here I am, slow and leisurely mellowing.
I am old wine in this new bottle.

Memory *Du Jour*

I have a drawer full of ghosts,
forgotten photos with smiling faces
urging me to remember when—
I open the drawer and select
the memory *du jour.*
And there you are on a mountain day
grinning like the prince
in charge of this alpine place.

Come take my hand,
and we'll walk through the golden aspens,
along the cool mountain stream,
and descend to reality together,
surrounded by warmth and light,
the aura of our past.

A Window to the Sky

I need a window to the sky
where I can float through the clouds,
and feel the wind blowing secrets,
a flight of song birds my companions.
I can hear the music of a summer night,
the rhythm of rain and rumbling thunder.

I need an unlocked door
so I can touch the trees
in the spring-flowered woods,
be warmed by sun-glowed dunes,
and know the challenging miracles
of the tangled web of life.

I need a place where I can
wonder and wander untrapped
by walls and time and reverie.
Here I can breathe the sunlit air
And wisely dance with hope,
my spirit free and unfettered.

My View in the Woods

This is my everyday view in the woods.
It changes as I sit in this shady enclave,
thinking I might peruse another chapter,
while the light shifts, wind-blown and green.

I can see the pathway ahead slipping out of sight.
I know where it goes, I've walked that way
only to return to my everyday place,
my customary thoughts and views in the woods.

I wonder where there is a trail that leads
beyond the confines of this small grove.
I've been cocooned here such a long time,
I truly need a short cut out of my thicket.

Autumnal Avenue

I'm sitting here quietly
but I have been seen.
Chickadee whispers
Chee-a chee-chee chee.
Bluejay shrieks *thief thief.*
And there is rustling
in the yellow aspen leaves.
Perhaps the wind
that snatched the seasons away.
Perhaps. . . .
Perhaps I should move on.

The fading summer sun,
warm and peaceful,
shimmers a cascade
of golden leaves.
Must I move on?

A tawny deer bolts
across the path,

white flag held high,
racing on to an untried trail,
fleeing, flying, breathless--
Perhaps I too will move on,
on to the unseen autumnal avenue.
Perhaps. . . .
Perhaps.

Kinship

I followed the road
through old Allegheny Mountains,
white-starred and spring green,
with stone barns,
and useful.
Stone houses, beautiful and warm
With two-hundred years of families.
There was a farm pond,
round and neat.
On one shore, young men,
clean shaven
white shirted with flat black hats,
jostling one another
as all young men do.
And a young woman,
aloof but watching.
The distance was great
but did we share an old kinship?

Plain green dress and braided hair,
        beautiful in the warm old Allegheny Valley,
Could we have known one another?

Another year, another road,
        The Pennsylvania 'Pike spins along
        through old mountains
        and new towns
        laid out before me.
There at the coffee shop,
        a young woman, plain blue dress,
        lace *kapp* in place,
        sensible shoes
        so like my grandmotherly brogues.
Our eyes meet and we smile
        in knowing kinship
        over our caramel lattes
        with double whipped cream.

Viola Knows

Viola knows beach stones,
smooth, water-worn,
and fragile white shells.
See, there under the birch tree
a mystic cairn:
three stones and a white shell
    holding a secret.

A secret, a mystery here?
Here in the front yard?
There's no mist nor darkness here.
There's nothing concealed
in a small white shell
    that we can see.

Viola knows beach stones
and shells and mysteries.
She is a sprite in a ruffled dress,
she silver-scooters her spells

to Grandpa's house
in cold March rain.
She is a glorious horse
galloping on a secret mission
to the mulberry tree.
She is a sorceress at seven.
    Viola knows.

A Lily Grows

A Lily grows by the linden tree
gathering beauty as she swings
from childhood to dreams.

A Lily grows singing and swinging
toward the music within her,
songs of the season and more.

A Lily grows swinging her way
toward her someday home,
finding her way to womanhood.

Weaver

I searched among my crewel yarns
to match your natural wools.
I could mend the small tear in your rug,
but I could not match the strength of your fibers.
I could blend the colors but the beauty
from your weaving hands eludes me.

Fourth of July in Flagstaff,
your granddaughter's granddaughter
in turquoise and jeans,
with generations of beauty before her
and beauty around her,
dances of yesterday and tomorrow.

To Tell Your Story

I see your slim hands and
know you are a woman
reaching beyond the cave wall
to tell your story.
Real hands in a joyous pattern
for eight hundred years,
hands discovering,
uncovering your reality.

Who among you imagined
the two Big Men and
the Woman with Child?
The ominous cluster
of dark hand prints
tell a story we'll never know.

Another hand carved the
timeless elk and big-horned sheep,
forever roaming the rocky walls.

And what conjuror drew
the graceful spirals?
What mystical story do they tell?

What wall will my hands
dance across to tell my story?

Among Women

Company houses, stark, dark
with dust of coal and slag.
Hail Mary!
Backyard clothesline sag
gray beneath the workday load,
Full of grace.
Black dust shadow,
Slag heap encroaching.
Blessed art thou,
surrounding without pollution
a coal town's absolution
Among women,
the bird bath shrine of Mary,
miraculous blue-gowned Mary.
Where are You?

In the season...

In the season of sunshine and strawberries
we talked of our womanly matters:
        of children and shortcake,
        of husbands and hopes,
        of slipcovers and strawberries---
And all was lucid and lovely.

In this season of strawberries
we talked of other matters:
        of forgotten and following fears,
        of clouds and veils,
        of a circling search---
And the strawberries were gone beyond.

In the season beyond and following
the unsaid thoughts emerge
        of unseen walls,
        of unheard hopes
        of your soul's unseating.
Will the strawberries again be sweet?

Dear Night Wandering Soul,

Your 4 a.m. call woke me,
frightened me.
When your tired fingers
dialed my number
the phone ID said
"Nursing Home ,"
and your sad voice said,
"Call me, call me."

I don't know you
but I could have been kind
when I said,
"Wrong number.
Do not call again."
And you said,
"Call me, call me."

Who would answer my
night wandering call?

My Own Song

I still have my voice
To sing a song
To state my mind.

I still have my mind
To solve a problem,
To choose my way.

I still have my way
To find the just,
To seek what's right.

I still have my right
To be and know myself,
To sing my true song.

Honest Advice

It's wise to be cautious:
Brush your teeth and eat your veggies.
Exercise and keep your shoestrings tied.
Look both ways before crossing the street.
Keep your credit card number to yourself.

There's wisdom in planning ahead:
Pay your bills on time—or in advance.
Charge your phone before it's dead.
Get to the grocery store prior to the next storm.
Order pizza before the beer is all gone.

Wisely choose words and symbols:
Say please and thank you.
Avoid placing foot in mouth.
Be honestly gracious and kind.
Cherish the owl on your shoulder.
Then boldly throw prudence to the winds of chance
And with heart on sleeve, wisely say *I love you*.

The Race

You know the story
of the tortoise and the hare.
Have you ever wondered
who really won that race?

Was it one of us,
the grizzle-haired tortoises
working our missing cores
with fifteen achy leg lifts
and balky bicep curls?

Did youth, that elusive rabbit,
hop along this way,
just beyond our seasoned reach?
Could we catch that teasing gray hare?

Maybe we galumphing turtles,
seeking our hazy youth,
spun our graceless wheels
over the fractious finish line.

Dear Person Reclining into My Lap on the Flight,

Wasn't Hawaii a perfect place to linger –
The warmth of the sand and music filling the nights,
the flowers and foods a fragrant blur.

So why did you bolt that rotten fish,
now your purple burps?
Why are you so fatigued
at the end of your vacation in paradise
that you can't sit up?

Would that you could burrow under the seats,
squirm out the door and thrash through the night.
Please be a solitary vagrant on your next flight
and cancel your frequent flyer miles.

Yours,
The hapless one you breathed on

Pranzo Speciale

The tour bus grinds to a stop.
The Verona *piazza* swirls with people
heading for a clamorous *ristorante,*
quick lunch before the thirty-minute,
round-trip walk to view Juliet's *casa,*
complete with balcony—and gift shop.

We shrug our dismissive shrugs
and amble down a quiet street.
There beneath our feet,
a sign inviting us downstairs.
Pranzo speciale
Pomodoro con basilica
e mozzarella

We gladly miss the Juliet hike
for lunch in this welcoming *trattoria.*
A heaping platter of juicy, red tomatoes,
fragrant, green sprigs of basil,
fresh, creamy mozzarella,
chunks of crisp bread, cold *birra,*

And the lunch-time violinist
plays love songs for us,
the intrepid Romeo and Juliet,
sans suicide and balcony.
Molte grazie, pomodoro con basilica.
Grazie mille, downstairs *trattoria.*

Do You Play Bridge?

Dear What's-Your-Name,
You probably don't remember me either,
but I think of you every time I am asked,
"Do you play bridge?"
We were in our twenties
when vastly pregnant Marion
and her teddy-bear husband,
invited us for a blind date
playing bridge at their home.

Everyone knew I was a bridge-beginner
and said they would guide my hand.
The game began quietly, but then
you asked if I knew the names of the suits
and understood the relative values
of the various cards.
I, who had grown up playing penny-ante Poker,
Hearts, Canasta, and Gin Rummy,
smiled sweetly and, with tongue firmly in cheek,
pointed out the black *shamrocks* card
that had just been played.

Despite the poisonous glare, the game went on
until I truly played the wrong card.
You swore at me, not at the cards.
You pounded on the table setting the cards flying,
and the teddy-bear showed you the door.
Somehow, I have survived bridgeless all these years.
Although you'll never receive this letter,
I'd really like to know if you are
a Grand Master of Solitaire and
how do you like playing the slots at the casino.

Yours,

An Abridged Gamer

If By Chance

I would be shocked if
by some remote chance
I had won the lottery
and could spend thousands
on worthy causes
of which there are too many.

I would be elated if
by some birding chance
the ivory-billed woodpecker
chose my bird feeder
for its afternoon snack
and I have photos for proof.

I would be jubilant if
by some popular chance
our elected politicians
served all of our nation
respectfully and wisely
as statesmen and stateswomen.

I would really be surprised if
by some genetic chance
I lived beyond one hundred
and still was with it,
but so far, so good,
and who's counting anyway?

Fourth of July Fireworks

Explosions large and small.
Flaming stars sizzling into the air.
Red
Green
Gold
Silver
Stars and whirligigs,
acrid smoke,
and then the show is over.
Are the celebrations adequate
Pursuits of Happiness?
Do effervescent and short-lived
stars equate our fragile
Life and Liberty?
If it is Self-evident that
All People are Created Equal,
why do those
Unalienable Rights
have to be redefined endlessly?
And still I hope for
Unity from Sea to Shining Sea.

This Real World

Here we sit laughing
Avoiding
Pretending
Disdaining

Fearful
Unforgiving

Faraway fires cloud our skies.
Icebergs melt and winds
revisit our flooding shores.
Children are crying,
death is in the air
hidden by blustering omission.

And here we sit
Observing
Questioning

Fearful

Seeking

We toast each other

with our cups of kindness,

tears for our losses,

marches for the dead,

and love for our world.

Here we are

Guarding

Protecting

Sheltering

We foil the fools who deny us

as we shield this real world

we live in.

Imagine

Imagine that pots of gold really
did exist at the foot of the rainbow –
Would there be traffic jams, fist fights,
portable security fences and guards,
lotteries and winners and losers?
Would leprechauns be chuckling
at the nonsense while hiding
away in their fairy forts?

Suppose Peter Pan really was successful
at guiding boys to Never-Never Land –
Would women and girls become
the real Rulers of the Universe,
the CEOs in charge of everything,
the recognized leaders who do not
take notes and fetch coffee?
Oh, and what would happen
to the next generation, if there were one?
Take note, Peter Pan, and plan carefully.

Imagine what would happen if suddenly
the skin color of the racists in our midst
would change — Would insights occur?
would histories be rewritten, cultures be revamped?
Would laws be written to acknowledge
the changes and challenges set forth?
Or would the same old skewed view of
human beings just take on a different hue?

Imagine what would happen if the common good,
if it really happens, was paid forward
and the Golden Rule was everyone's expectation.
Imagine who would be in charge
and how they would lead.
Imagine the many colors in that rainbow
and the treasures found at its foot.
How will those many treasures be distributed?
And how does this actually work in reality?

Love

In my world, love blooms
with early purple crocus,
the smell of spring rain,
the warmth of sand
in the summer sun,
your hand in mine.

My world sings exuberantly
of love and mountain streams,
thunder's music and children's songs,
a dance for the New Year,
and your voice in celebration.

In my archival world,
I awaken with you
on a rainy morning
remembering the stars.

The Gift Box

Have you ever received
an intriguing but empty box?
Because it was my birthday,
I was puzzled by this unfilled box.

I took a second, scathing look
and there on the starkly plain lid
was this rather curt message:
"Fill me."

The inside was totally bare
but brightly lined with blue paper.
There was another pointed message:
"Place gifts here."

I wonder what sort of gifts
should be put in this unexpected box?
I've received many gifts, many times,
some to keep, some to give away.

So here's my camera and its mission
to record a multitude of gifts:
my children and grandchildren,
the beautiful world, and my loves.

Here's the tattered *Wizard of Oz*,
my well-loved book, a part of
my parents' legacy of reading
that fills my treasured shelves.

This shamrock, a descendant
from my mother's thriving plants,
promises sought-after good luck
and ample beauty to discover.

Mütta's tiny reading glasses
tell Great Grandmother's story.
Here's the gift of many generations,
their boundless courage and fidelity.

Here's the family recipe collection
including our special goulash soup,

the standard dish for cold weather
and warm family homecomings.

A Petoskey stone and an agate,
remnants of sun-splashed lake days,
complete with children, water, sand,
and ample time for enduring dreams.

My wedding ring could add
a long love story, shared ventures,
endless conversations, and---
No, I'll always wear this ring.

My old violin needs some repairs,
but it's filled with music memories.
The joys of being part of music
could fill this blue-lined box.

I'm not finished with this gift box.
I'll keep the box open and welcoming.
Thanks to this surprising gift of Time,
I'm finding forgotten and lost gifts.

The Gift of Song

Thank you, Lord, for the gift of song
that brings us together in harmony,
in laughter and in tears,
in friendship and with joy!
We clap our hands and shout out loud:
O magnify the Lord with me.
Magnificat, magnificat anima mea Dominum.

Thank you, Lord, for the gift of music
as it animates our lives and souls
through lullabies and love songs,
through beauty, inspiration, and songs of praise.
O bless the Lord my soul.
All that is in me bless his Holy name.
Et exultavit spiritus meus in Deo salutary meo.

Thank you Lord for the gift of friends.
Intercede pro devoto populo.
And bless this gift of song.
Hosanna in excelsis.
Amen, amen, amen.

Acknowledgements

Special thanks to Wilma Kahn, instructor, and members of the Creative Writing class. Your comments and support have cheered me on.

"Winter Sun" was first published in *Encore Magazine: Southwest Michigan's Magazine,* February 2014, page 41. "Sentinels," "Solstice," and "Tomorrow" were published in various issues of *The Villager,* 2019-2021, monthly, in-house newsletter, Friendship Village, Senior Living Community, Kalamazoo, Michigan. The opening lines of "Sentinels," *Over my head, I hear music in the air,* are lyrics from an African American spiritual.

"There Should Be Stars" was written in celebration of our 58th anniversary. "Lake Song" is dedicated to the memory of our daughter, Gail Cordier Kroske, 1960-2013. "When I Think of Home" is based on the thoughts shared by members of the Kalamazoo Community Chorale as they prepared a concert on the theme of Home. This poem and "The Gift of Song" are dedicated to the Chorale. "The Gift of Song" has been set to choral music composed by Nancy Ford Charles.

Made in the USA
Monee, IL
29 September 2022